Going Fast

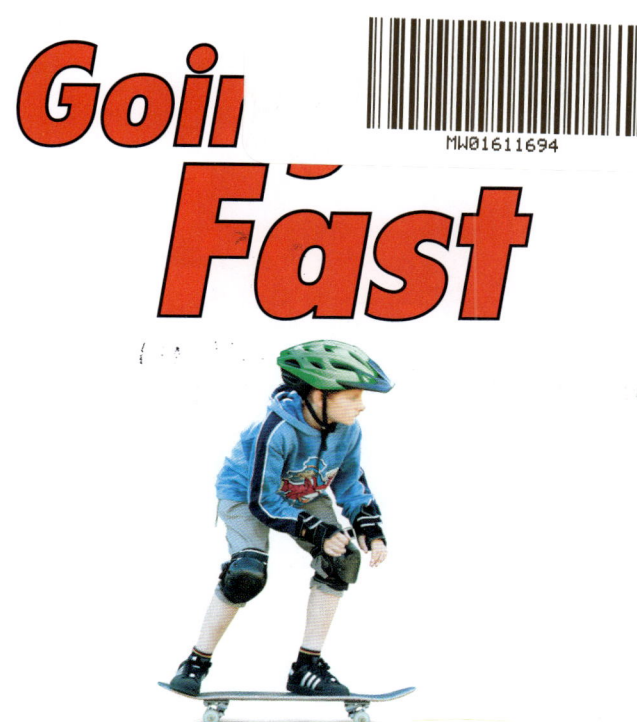

by Robert Newell

 HOUGHTON MIFFLIN   BOSTON

PHOTOGRAPHY CREDITS: Cover © Robert Michael/CORBIS; Toc © Siegfried Kuttig/Alamy; 2 © Robert Michael/CORBIS; 3 © Siegfried Kuttig/Alamy; 4-5 © Transtock; 6 © Veer; 7 © David R. Frazier Photolibrary, Inc./Alamy; 8 © Veer; 9 © Transtock; 10 © Image Farm Inc./Alamy

Printed in China

ISBN-13: 978-0-547-01703-7
ISBN-10: 0-547-01703-0

4 5 6 7 8 9 0940 15 14 13 12 11 10

Look at the bike.
It can go fast.

Look at the <mark>skateboard</mark>.
It can go fast.
The boy has a helmet
and pads to be safe.

Look at the <mark>motorcycle.</mark>
It can go fast.
Two people can ride
on it.

Look at the boat.
It can go fast
in the water.

Look at the cars.
They can go very fast.

Look at the trucks.
Trucks can go fast, too.
Big trucks go fast
on big roads.

Look at the airplane.
It can go fast.
And it can go
up, up, up.

Look at the race cars.
They can go fast.
They can go around
and around.

Look at this race car.
It can **not** go fast!

Responding

Text and Graphic Features How do the words go with the pictures on each page of the book?

Write About It

Text to World Draw a picture of something that can go fast. Label your picture. Then write a sentence about it.

WORDS TO KNOW

to

LEARN MORE WORDS

motorcycle | **skateboard**

TARGET SKILL **Text and Graphic Features** Tell how words go with photos.

TARGET STRATEGY **Question** Ask questions about what you are reading.

GENRE **Informational text** gives facts about a topic.